Diary

Code

A	2	N	╲
B	(	O	5
C	)	P	+
D	o	Q	‖
E	3	R	P
F	v	S	=
G	n	T	~
H	ℓ	U	6
I	4	V	𝓰
J	4	W	8
K	I	X	w
L	ᔑ	Y	7
M	—	Z	9

bb	€	nn	⅄
cc	ℨ	pp	ⱦ
ch	▽	tt	⅄
ee	;	sh	∧
ff	Φ	ss	?
ll	:	th	✓
oo	!	rr	₽

Mr	✕	Miss	✕
Mrs	✕	and	✕

Word	Symbol	Word	Symbol
About	2(56~	Meet	-ȝ~
All	2:	More	-5P3
Also	2ᴆ=5	New	\38
As	2=	Now	\58
At	2~	One	5\3
Be	(3	Other	5√3P
But	(6~	See	=;
By	(7	She	∧3
Can	)2\	Take	~2\3
Could	)56ᴆo	That	√2~
Date	o2~3	Their	√34P
Drink	oP4\l	They	√37
Eat	32~	This	√4=
Find	∨4\o	Very	ȝ3P7
For	∨5P	Want	82\~
Get	∩3~	Week	8;l
Girl	∩4Pᴆ	Went	83\~
Have	Q2ȝ3	What	8Q2~
Her	Q3P	Will	84:
Him	Q4-	With	84√
How	Q58	Woman	85-2\
Into	4\~5	Would	856ᴆo
Know	l\58	Yes	73=
Like	ᴆ4l3	You	756
Make	-2l3	Your	756P

Made in the USA
Monee, IL
04 April 2020